50 STATES TO CELEBRATE

Celebrating
WASHINGTON
STATE

The text of this book is set in Weidemann.
The display type is set in Bernard Gothic.
The illustrations are drawn with pencil and colored digitally.
The maps are pen and ink, and watercolor.

Photograph of goldfinch on page 32 © 2013 by William Leaman/Alamy
Photograph of trout on page 32 © 2013 by © Kletr/Shutterstock
Photograph of rhododendron on page 32 © 2013 by photolibrary

Library of Congress Cataloging-in-Publication Data
Bauer, Marion Dane.
Celebrating Washington / Marion Dane Bauer ; illustrated by C.B. Canga.
p. cm. — (50 states to celebrate) (Green light readers. Level 3)
ISBN: 978-0-544-28967-3 paper over board
ISBN: 978-0-544-28948-2 trade paper
1. Washington (State)—Juvenile literature. I. Canga, C. B., illustrator. II. Title.
F891.3.B38 2014
979.7—dc23

Manufactured in China
SCP 10 9 8 7 6 5 4 3 2 1
4500471644

50 STATES TO CELEBRATE

Celebrating
WASHINGTON
STATE

Written by **Marion Dane Bauer**
Illustrated by **C. B. Canga**

Green Light Readers
Houghton Mifflin Harcourt
Boston   New York

Hi! I'm Mr. Geo.

Here I am in the **Evergreen** State.

That's a nickname for the state of Washington.

I'll bet you can guess why.

Washington is the only state named after a president.

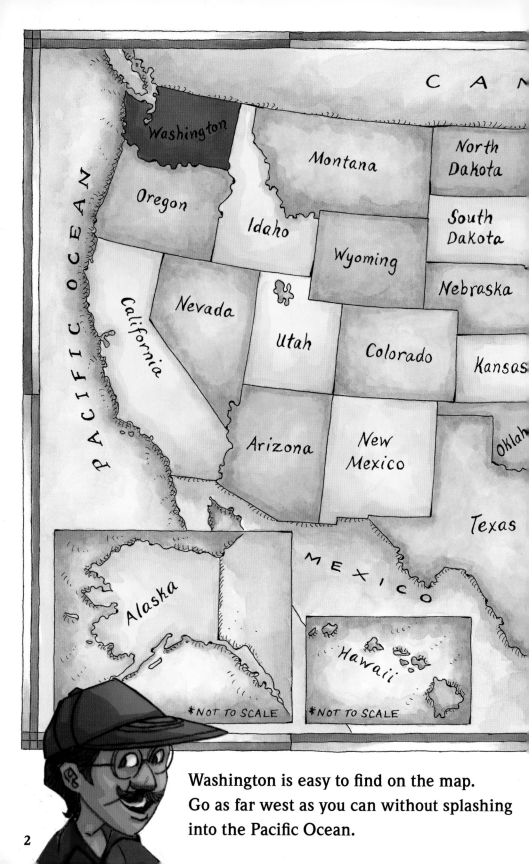

Washington is easy to find on the map.
Go as far west as you can without splashing
into the Pacific Ocean.

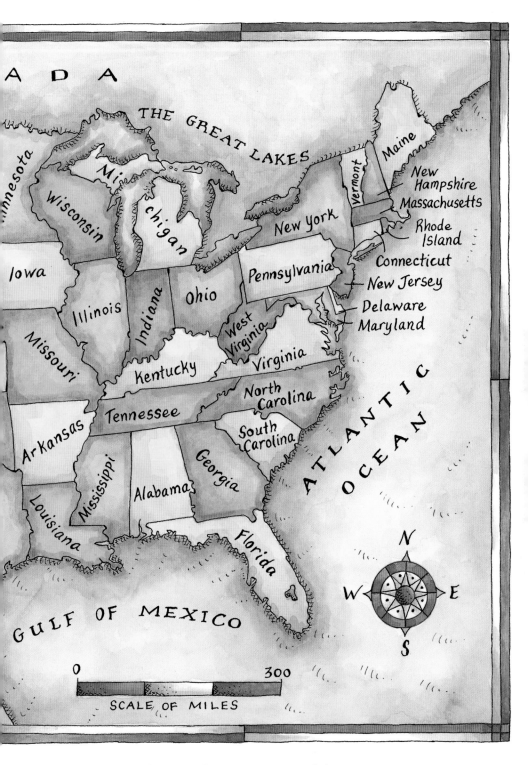

Now go as far north as you can without
crossing into Canada.
There it is! That's Washington.

Olympic National Park is like three parks in one.
It has mountains, forest, and seashore.
Let's start our visit at Hurricane Ridge.

The rare Roosevelt elk lives in Olympic National Park. So do deer, black bears, and cougars.

This park ranger is going to take us
on a hike through the forest.
If I spy all the things on my nature list,
I can call myself a Junior Ranger.
Wish me luck!

Today we're exploring another part of this immense park, the Hoh Rain Forest. Look at those towering trees and all the hanging moss! It's beautiful *and* mysterious.

I'm going to hike all the way to the Blue **Glacier**.

This llama will carry my gear.

Isn't he cute?

There are about 250 glaciers in Olympic National Park.

Now let's go to the coast.

Tide pools.

Sandy beaches.

Rocky cliffs.

This park has it all!

More wonders wait in the salty waters to the north. Look what found me while I was paddling around **Orcas** Island!

Sea kayaking, biking, hiking, and bird watching make the San Juan Islands a favorite vacation spot.

Let's go to the city of Seattle next.
There's nothing like the Space Needle.
It looks like a flying saucer up there!

There's so much to do here at Seattle Center.

We can ride the **monorail**.

We can watch a laser show.

We can visit a glass flower garden,

or experience music at the EMP Museum.

Am I too old to be a rock star?

Seattle Center was originally built for the 1962 World's Fair. Today it is still a park and an arts and entertainment center.

It's fun riding to the top of the Space Needle.
What luck that we're visiting on a clear day.
Seattle doesn't get too many of those.
Look! We can see all the way to Mount Rainier!

Seattle took its name from a Native American Indian leader who became friendly with the European settlers.

At Pike Place Market we can buy fresh food direct from the farmers.

People sell flowers here too, and crafts of all kinds.

Musicians entertain.

So do puppets.

Watch out! The fish tossers are at it again!

Did you know?

Farmers have been selling their produce at Pike Place Market since 1907.

15

People from many different cultures and parts of the
world live in Washington.

In May, thousands gather for the annual
Northwest Folklife Festival.

They bring their stories, music, and customs.

I love to dance!

Come join the fun!

Wherever I go, I root for the hometown teams.
In Seattle that would be the Mariners for baseball
and the Seahawks for football.

Some of the world's fastest motorboats
race on Lake Washington at a summer
event called Seafair.

The Cascade Mountain Range looms large
in Washington.
It divides the state into two different climates.
To the west, the days are often cool and wet.
To the east, the weather is warmer and drier.

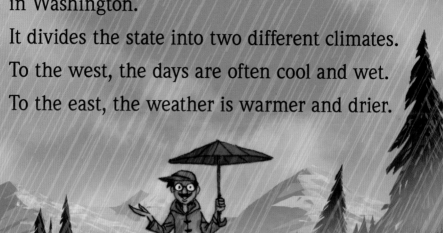

Seattle gets about 149 days of rain a year.
The city of Yakima gets about 72.

The Cascades are home to five active **volcanoes.**
I'm glad I wasn't here in 1980 when
Mount St. Helens erupted.
But I love biking in the blast zone now!

Rich land and natural resources helped
early Native American communities grow.
Rivers filled with **salmon** fed people well.
Tall trees provided wood for canoes and homes.
Beaver fur and deer **hide** gave warmth in winter.

Today, Washington is home to more than
30 different Native American tribes.

Some Native Americans groups held large festivals called **potlatches.**

Many carved **totem poles** to tell their family stories. I wonder what my story would look like carved into a pole!

The first Europeans came here to find
new sea routes and spread religion.
They admired the good land and natural resources,
especially valuable beaver **pelts**.
Many settled and developed new ways of life.

Today I'm visiting a restored fur-trading village at Fort Vancouver.

Do I look silly in this old-fashioned hat?

The explorers Lewis and Clark first saw the Pacific Ocean from canoes on the Columbia River in 1805.

Fir, spruce, cedar, and pine trees.
The land in Washington produces dense forests.
Lumber has long been one of the state's main
industries.

Coal, copper, and gold are found here too.

And, of course, fishing has always been important.

Look what I caught for my dinner!

Even without much rain, eastern Washington is great for farming.

The Grand Coulee **Dam** makes much of it possible. The water held in its **reservoir** is used for **irrigation**. Washington is famous for growing fruits, especially apples, cherries, grapes, and pears.

Did you know?

Washington also grows a lot of wheat and vegetables, including potatoes and peas.

But what dazzles me most are rows and rows
of colorful tulips in full bloom!
They grow in northwestern Washington.

The waters of Puget **Sound** flow many miles inland. That means cities far from the Pacific coast can still be port cities.

Olympia, Tacoma, and Seattle are all exciting port cities on Puget Sound.

Great ocean liners bring in freight and carry more away.

Ferries carry passengers and cars across this saltwater highway.

Above all else, though, Washingtonians treasure the natural beauty of their state.

Snow-capped mountains.

Tumbling streams.

Towering trees.

Abundant wildlife.

Scenic Washington will always call me back!

Fast Facts About Washington

State motto: *Alki* ("Bye and Bye").

State capital: Olympia.

Year of statehood: 1889.

Other major cities: Seattle, Tacoma, Bellevue, Spokane, Yakima.

State bird: Willow goldfinch.

State fish: Steelhead trout.

State flower: Coast rhododendron.

State flag:

Population: According to the 2010 census, just under 7 million.

Fun fact: Washington is home to many big companies, including Boeing, which makes airplanes; Microsoft, which makes computer software; Starbucks, which sells coffee; and Amazon, which sells books.

Dates in Washington History

1500s: Many different Native American tribes are living in the region.

1775: Spanish explorers become the first Europeans to land in Washington.

1792: Robert Gray locates and sails into the mouth of the Columbia River and claims the area for the United States.

1805: Lewis and Clark follow the Columbia River to the Pacific coast.

1842: Pioneers start using the Oregon Trail to migrate to the Washington area.

1851: Seattle founded.

1853: Washington territory established.

1883: The Northern Pacific Railroad connects St. Paul, Minnesota, with Tacoma, Washington.

1889: Washington becomes the 42nd state; the Great Seattle Fire destroys much of the city.

1942: The Grand Coulee Dam completed.

1962: The World's Fair is held in Seattle, triggering the construction of Seattle Center.

1980: Mount St. Helens experiences a major eruption.

2012: Seattle Center opens Chihuly Garden and Glass, featuring colorful glass sculptures by Dale Chihuly, an artist from Tacoma, Washington.

Activities

1. **LOCATE** the states that border Washington on the map on pages 2 and 3. Which state is to the south? Which state is to the east? **SAY** each state's name out loud.

2. **DESIGN** a small poster about fun things to see and do in Washington. Include words and picture in your poster.

3. **SHARE** two facts you learned about Washington with a family member or friend.

4. **PRETEND** you are a contestant on a TV game show. The host is going to ask you five questions about Washington. If you answer correctly, you will win the game.

   a. **WHERE** in Washington can you find Roosevelt elk?

   b. **WHAT** mountain can you see from the Space Needle?

   c. **WHEN** did Mount St. Helens experience its most recent major eruption?

   d. **WHO** were the American explorers who first saw the Pacific Ocean from canoes on the Columbia River in 1805?

5. **UNJUMBLE** these words that have something to do with Washington. Write your answers on a separate sheet of paper.

   a. **CARO** (HINT: A water animal)

   b. **RVAEBE** (HINT: A furry animal)

   c. **ANRIREI** (HINT: A mountain)

   d. **SERRNEVEEG** (HINT: They grow in forests)

   FOR ANSWERS, SEE PAGE 36.

Glossary

dam: a barrier built across a waterway to control the flow of water or to create a lake for storing water. (p. 26)

evergreen: a tree or bush that has green leaves or needles all year. (p. 1)

glacier: a thick, heavy mass of slowly moving ice. (p. 7)

irrigation: a way of supplying land or crops with water using streams, ditches, pipes, or sprinklers. (p. 26)

hide: the thick, tough skin of an animal; hides can be used to make leather and suede. (p. 20)

lumber: wood from trees that is sawed into boards and beams. (p. 24)

monorail: a train system that operates on one track or rail; the train cars hang from or balance on the rail. (p. 11)

orcas: black and white dolphins; Orcas Island is the largest of the San Juan Islands in northwestern Washington. (p. 9)

pelt: an animal skin with the fur still on it; beaver pelts were once used to make hats, especially top hats. (p. 22)

potlatch: a Native American ceremony or festival. (p. 21)

reservoir: a pond or lake that is used for storing water. (p. 26)

salmon: a type of fish with a silvery body and pinkish flesh; salmon live in oceans but swim up rivers to lay their eggs in fresh water. (p. 20)

sound: a long, wide inlet of an ocean. Puget Sound, located in Washington State, is a deep inlet of the Pacific Ocean. (p. 28)

totem pole: a pole that is carved with images of animals, plants, or natural objects that symbolize a family of Native American culture; the images, also called totems, are usually stacked one on top of another. (p. 21)

volcano: an opening in the earth's crust through which lava, ash, and hot gases can escape. (p. 19)

Answers to activities on page 34:

1) Oregon is to the south; Idaho is to the east; 2) Posters will vary; 3) Answers will vary; 4a) Olympic National Park, 4b) Mount Rainier, 4c) 1980, 4d) Lewis and Clark; 5a) ORCA, 5b) BEAVER, 5c) RAINIER, 5d) EVERGREENS.